In the Year 1958

by

Kerry Butters.

In the Year 1958

Millennium:	**2nd millennium**
Centuries:	19th century – **20th century** – 21st century
Decades:	1920s 1930s 1940s – 1950s – **1960s** 1970s 1980s
Years:	1955 1956 1957 – **1958** – 1959 1960 1961

1958 (MCMLVIII) was a common year starting on Wednesday (dominical letter E) of the Gregorian calendar, the 1958th year of the Common Era (CE) and *Anno Domini* (AD) designations, the 958th year of the 2nd millennium, the 58th year of the 20th century, and the 9th year of the 1950s decade.

Contents

Events

January

- January 1
  - The European Economic Community (EEC) is founded.
  - The first Carrefour store opens, in Annecy.
- January 3 – Edmund Hillary's Commonwealth Trans-Antarctic Expedition completes the third overland journey to the South Pole, and the first to use powered vehicles.
- January 4 – Sputnik 1 (launched on October 4, 1957) falls to Earth from its orbit and burns up.
- January 8 – 14-year-old Bobby Fischer wins the United States Chess Championship.
- January 18
  - Armed Lumbee Indians confront a handful of Klansmen in Maxton, North Carolina.
  - The first of Leonard Bernstein's *Young People's Concerts* with the New York Philharmonic is telecast by CBS. The Emmy-winning series (one concert approximately every three months except for the summer) will run for more than fourteen years. It will

make Bernstein's name a household word, and the most famous conductor in the U.S.

- January 20 – Anne de Vries releases the fourth and final volume of *Journey Through the Night*.
- January 28
  - Hall of Fame baseball player Roy Campanella is involved in an automobile accident that ends his career and leaves him paralyzed.
  - Godtfred Kirk Christiansen files a patent for the iconic plastic Lego brick. Since its foundation, the company has made an enormous 400 billion Lego elements.
- January 31 – The first successful American satellite, Explorer 1, is launched into orbit.

February

- February 1 – Egypt and Syria unite to form the United Arab Republic.
- February 2 – The word *Aerospace* is coined, from the words Aircraft (aero) and Spacecraft (space), taking into consideration that the Earth's atmosphere and outerspace is to be one, or a single realm.
- February 5
  - Gamal Abdel Nasser is nominated as the first president of the United Arab Republic.
  - The Tybee Bomb, a 7,600 pound (3,500 kg) Mark 15 hydrogen bomb, is lost in the waters off Savannah, Georgia.
- February 6 – Seven Manchester United footballers are among the 21 people killed in the Munich air disaster in West Germany, on the return flight from a European Cup game in Yugoslavia. 23 people survive, but four of them, including manager Matt Busby and players Johnny Berry

and Duncan Edwards, are in a serious condition. Busby and Berry would pullthrough although Berry would never play again. Edwards died fortnight later.

- February 11
  - The strongest ever known solar maximum is recorded.
  - Marshal Chen Yi succeeds Zhou Enlai as Chinese Minister of Foreign Affairs.
  - Ruth Carol Taylor is the first African American woman hired as a flight attendant. Hired by Mohawk Airlines, her career lasts only six months, due to another discriminatory barrier – the airline's ban on married flight attendants.
- February 14 – The Hashemite Kingdoms of Iraq and Jordan unite in the Arab Federation with King Faisal II of Iraq as head of state.
- February 17 – Pope Pius XII declares Saint Clare the patron saint of television.
- February 20 – A test rocket explodes at Cape Canaveral.
- February 21 – A peace symbol is designed and completed by Gerald Holtom, commissioned by the Campaign for Nuclear Disarmament, in protest against the Atomic Weapons Research Establishment.
- February 23
  - Cuban rebels kidnap five-time world driving champion Juan Manuel Fangio, releasing him 28 hours later.
  - Arturo Frondizi is elected president of Argentina.
- February 24 – In Cuba, Fidel Castro's *Radio Rebelde* begins broadcasting from Sierra Maestra.
- February 25 – Bertrand Russell launches the Campaign for Nuclear Disarmament.
- February 28 – One of the worst school bus accidents in U.S. history occurs at Prestonburg, Kentucky; 27 are killed.

March

- March 1 – The Turkish passenger ship *Üsküdar* capsizes and sinks in the Gulf of İzmit, Turkey; at least 300 die.
- March 2 – A British Commonwealth Trans-Antarctic Expedition team led by Sir Vivian Fuchs completes the first overland crossing of the Antarctic, using snowcat caterpillar tractors and dogsled teams, in 99 days, via the South Pole.
- March 8 – The USS *Wisconsin* is decommissioned, leaving the United States Navy without an active battleship for the first time since 1896 (it is recommissioned October 22, 1988).
- March 11 – A U.S. B-47 bomber accidentally drops an atom bomb on Mars Bluff, South Carolina. Without a fissile warhead, its conventional explosives destroy a house and injure several people.
- March 17 – The Convention on the Inter-Governmental Maritime Consultative Organization (IMCO) enters into force, founding the IMCO as a specialized agency of the United Nations.
- March 17 – The United States launches the Vanguard 1 satellite.
- March 19 – The Monarch Underwear Company fire occurs in New York, killing twenty-four.
- March 24 – The U.S. Army inducts Elvis Presley, transforming The King Of Rock & Roll into U.S. Private #53310761.
- March 25 – Canada's Avro Arrow makes its debut flight.
- March 26
  - The United States Army launches Explorer 3.

- The 30th Academy Awards ceremony takes place; *The Bridge on the River Kwai* wins seven awards, including Academy Award for Best Picture.
- March 27 – Nikita Khrushchev becomes Premier of the Soviet Union.

April

- April – Unemployment in Detroit reaches 20%, marking the height of the Recession of 1958 in the United States.
- April 1 – The BBC Radiophonic Workshop is established.
- April 3 – Castro's revolutionary army begins its attacks on Havana.
- April 4 – April 7 – In the first protest march for the Campaign for Nuclear Disarmament from Hyde Park, London to Aldermaston, Berkshire, demonstrators demand the banning of nuclear weapons.
- April 4 – Cheryl Crane, daughter of actress Lana Turner, fatally stabs her mother's gangster lover Johnny Stompanato (the stabbing is eventually ruled as self-defense).
- April 6 – Soraya Esfandiary-Bakhtiari divorces the Shah of Iran, Mohammad Reza Pahlavi after she is unable to produce any children.
- April 14
  - The satellite Sputnik 2 (launched 3 November 1957) disintegrates during reentry from orbit.
  - Van Cliburn wins the International Tchaikovsky Competition for pianists in Moscow, breaking Cold War tensions.
- April 15 – The San Francisco Giants beat the Los Angeles Dodgers 8–0 at San Francisco's Seals Stadium, in the first

Major League Baseball regular season game ever played in California.

- April 17 – King Baudouin of Belgium officially opens the world's fair in Brussels, also known as Expo 58. The Atomium forms the centrepiece.
- April 20 – The Montreal Canadiens win the Stanley Cup after defeating the Boston Bruins in six games.
- April 21 – United Airlines Flight 736 is involved in a mid-air collision with a U.S. Air Force F-100F jet fighter near Las Vegas. All 49 persons in both aircraft are killed.

May

- May 1
  - Arturo Frondizi becomes President of Argentina.
  - The Nordic Passport Union comes into force.
- May 9 – Actor-singer Paul Robeson, whose passport has been reinstated, sings in a sold-out one-man recital at Carnegie Hall. The recital is such a success that Robeson gives another one at Carnegie Hall a few days later; but, after this, Robeson is seldom seen in public in the United States again. His Carnegie Hall concerts are later released on records and on CD.
- May 10 – Interviewed in the Chave d'Ouro café, when asked about his rival António de Oliveira Salazar, Humberto Delgado utters one of the most famous comments in Portuguese political history: "Obviamente, demito-o! (Obviously, I'll sack him!)".
- May 12 – A formal North American Aerospace Defense Command agreement is signed between the United States and Canada.

- May 13
  - French Algerian protesters seize government offices in Algiers, leading to a military coup.
  - During a visit to Caracas, Venezuela, Vice President Richard Nixon's car is attacked by anti-American demonstrators.
- May 15
  - The Soviet Union launches Sputnik 3.
  - MGM's *Gigi* opens in New York City, beginning its run in the U.S. after being shown at the Cannes film festival. The last of the great MGM musicals, it will become a huge critical and box office success and win nine Academy Awards including Best Picture. *Gigi* is Lerner and Loewe's first musical written especially for film, and is deliberately written in a style evoking the team's *My Fair Lady*, which was still playing on Broadway at the time and could not be filmed yet.
- May 18 – An F-104 Starfighter sets a world speed record of 1,404.19 mph (2,259.82 km/h).
- May 20 – Fulgencio Batista's government launches a counteroffensive against Castro's rebels.
- May 21 – United Kingdom Postmaster General Ernest Marples announces that from December, Subscriber Trunk Dialling will be introduced in the Bristol area.
- May 23 – Explorer 1 ceases transmission.
- May 28 – Real Madrid beats A.C.Milan 3-2 at Heysel Stadium, Brussels and wins the 1957-58 European Cup (football).
- May 30 – The bodies of unidentified United States soldiers killed in action during World War II and the Korean War are buried at the Tomb of the Unknowns in Arlington National Cemetery.

June

- June 1
  - Charles de Gaulle is brought out of retirement to lead France by decree for 6 months.
  - Iceland extends its fishing limits to 12 miles (22.2 km).
- a Murderer killed woman in Amityville, New York in her house while she was showering this event is based on 1960's movie psycho and 1998's remake
- June 2 – In San Simeon, California, Hearst Castle opens to the public for guided tours.
- June 4 – French President Charles de Gaulle visits Algeria.
- June 8 – The SS *Edmund Fitzgerald* is launched; she will be the largest Lake freighter for more than a dozen years.
- June 15 – Pizza Hut is founded.
- June 16 – Imre Nagy is hanged for treason in Hungary.
- June 20 – The iron barque *Omega* of Callao, Peru (built in Scotland, 1887), sinks on passage carrying guano from the Pachacamac Islands for Huacho, the world's last full-rigged ship trading under sail alone.
- June 27 – The Peronist party becomes legal again in Argentina.
- June 29 – Brazil beats Sweden 5–2 in the final game to win the football World Cup in Sweden.
- June 30 – The Ifni War ends.

July

- July 5 – Gasherbrum I, the 11th highest mountain in the world, is first ascended.

- July 7
  - United States President Dwight D. Eisenhower signs the Alaska Statehood Act into law.
  - The first International House of Pancakes (IHOP) opens in Toluca Lake, Los Angeles.
- July 9 – 1958 Lituya Bay megatsunami: A 7.8 Mw strike-slip earthquake in Southeast Alaska causes a landslide that produces a megatsunami. The runup from the waves reached 525 m (1,722 ft) on the rim of Lituya Bay.
- July 10 – The first parking meters are installed in Britain.
- July 11
  - Count Michael Rhédey von Kis-Rhéde, direct descendant of Samuel Aba, King of Hungary, at the age of 60 is pistol-whipped and murdered over a few hectares of land by Czechoslovak Communists during the collectivization process at his residence in Olcsvar, Slovakia.
  - Scottish serial killer Peter Manuel, "The Beast of Birkenshaw" is hanged at Barlinnie Prison in Glasgow for the murder of seven people.
- July 12
  - The Beatles, at the time known as The Quarrymen, pay 17 shillings and 6 pence to have their first recording session where they record Buddy Holly's "That'll Be the Day" and "In Spite of All the Danger", a song written by Paul McCartney and George Harrison.
  - Henri Cornelis becomes Governor-General of the Belgian Congo, the last Belgian governor prior to independence.
- July 14 – July 14 Revolution in Iraq. King Faisal is killed. Abdul Qassim assumes power.

- July 15 – In Lebanon, 5,000 United States Marines land in the capital Beirut in order to protect the pro-Western government there.
- July 17 – British paratroopers arrive in Jordan; King Hussein has asked help against pressure from Iraq.
- July 20 – Various rebel groups in Cuba join forces but the communists do not join them.
- July 24 – The first life peerage under the Life Peerages Act 1958 is created in the United Kingdom.
- July 26
  - Explorer program: Explorer 4 is launched.
  - Elizabeth II gives her son and heir apparent The Prince Charles the customary title of Prince of Wales.
- July 29 – The U.S. Congress formally creates the National Aeronautics and Space Administration (NASA).
- July 31 – The Tibetan resistance movement against rule by China receives support from the United States Central Intelligence Agency.

August

- August 1 – The last Tom and Jerry episode (*Tot Watchers*) made by William Hanna and Joseph Barbera is released. Tom and Jerry will not be released to theaters again until 1961.
- August 3 – The nuclear-powered submarine USS *Nautilus* becomes the first vessel to cross the North Pole under water.
- August 6 – Australian athlete Herb Elliott clips almost three seconds off the world record for the mile run at Santry Stadium, Dublin, recording a time of 3 minutes 54.5 seconds.

- August 14 – A 4-engine Lockheed L-1049 Super Constellation aircraft belonging to KLM crashes into the sea with 99 people on board.
- August 17 – The first Thor-Able rocket is launched, carrying Pioneer 0, from Cape Canaveral Air Force Station Space Launch Complex 17. The launch fails due to a first stage malfunction.
- August 18
  - Vladimir Nabokov's controversial novel *Lolita* is published in the United States.
  - Brojen Das from East Pakistan swims across the English Channel in a competition, as the first Bangali as well as the first Asian to ever do it. He is first among 39 competitors.
- August 23
  - Chinese Civil War: The Second Taiwan Strait Crisis begins with the People's Liberation Army's bombardment of Quemoy.
  - President of the United States Dwight D. Eisenhower signs the Federal Aviation Act, transferring all authority over aviation in the USA to the newly created Federal Aviation Agency (FAA, later renamed Federal Aviation Administration).
- August 27 – Operation Argus: The United States begins nuclear tests over the South Atlantic.
- August 30 – September 1 – Notting Hill race riots: Riots occur between blacks and whites in Notting Hill, London.

September

- September 1 – The first Cod War begins between the United Kingdom and Iceland.

- September 6 – Paul Robeson performs in concert at the Soviet Young Pioneer camp Artek.
- September 12 – Jack Kilby invents the first integrated circuit.
- September 14 – Two rockets designed by German engineer Ernst Mohr (the first German post-war rockets) reach the upper atmosphere.
- September 27
  - Typhoon Ida kills at least 1,269 in Honshū, Japan.
  - Hurricane Helene, the worst storm of the North Atlantic hurricane season, reaches category 4 status.
- September 28 – In France, a majority of 79% says yes to the constitution of the Fifth Republic.
- September 30 – The U.S.S.R. performs a nuclear test at Novaya Zemlya.

October

- October 1
  - Tunisia and Morocco join the Arab League.
  - NASA starts operations and replaces the NACA.
- October 2 – Guinea declares itself independent from France.
- October 4 – BOAC uses the new De Havilland Comet jets, to become the first airline to fly jet passenger services across the Atlantic.
- October 9 – Pope Pius XII dies.
- October 11 – Pioneer 1, the second and most successful of the 3 project Able space probes, becomes the first spacecraft launched by the newly formed NASA.
- October 13 – Penny Coelen is crowned as Miss World 1958 during the 8th Miss World pageant, the first South African to win the title.

- October 16 – First broadcast of the long-running BBC Television children's programme *Blue Peter*.
- October 19 – Beginning of Great Chinese Famine.
- October 21 – The Life Peerages Act entitles women to sit in the British House of Lords for the first time. The Baronesses Swanborough (Stella Isaacs, Marchioness of Reading) and Wooton (Barbara Wootton, Baroness Wootton of Abinger) are the first to take their seats.
- October 23 – Nobel Committee announces Boris Pasternak as the winner of the 1958 Prize for Literature
- October 26 – First transatlantic flight of a Pan American World Airways Boeing 707.
- October 28 – Pope John XXIII succeeds Pope Pius XII as the 261st pope.

November

- November 3 – The new UNESCO building is inaugurated in Paris.
- November 10 – The bossa nova is born in Rio de Janeiro, with João Gilberto's recording of *Chega de Saudade*.
- November 10 – Harry Winston donates the Hope Diamond to the Smithsonian Institution.
- November 18 – En route to Rogers City, Michigan, the lake freighter SS *Carl D. Bradley* breaks up and sinks in a storm on Lake Michigan; 33 of the 35 crewmen on board perish.
- November 22 – The Menzies Liberal government in Australia is re-elected for a fifth term.
- November 23 – The radio version of *Have Gun – Will Travel* premieres. It is one of the last dramas to go on the air on commercial radio. Only some NPR stations will broadcast radio dramas in years to come.

- November 25 – French Sudan gains autonomy as a self-governing member of the French colonial empire.
- November 28 – Chad, the Republic of the Congo, and Gabon become autonomous republics within the French colonial empire.
- November 30 – Gaullists win the French parliamentary election.

December

- December 1
    - Adolfo López Mateos takes office as President of Mexico.
    - Our Lady of the Angels School fire: At least 90 students and 3 nuns are killed in a fire in Chicago.
- December 5
    - Subscriber trunk dialling (STD) is inaugurated in the United Kingdom by the Queen, when she dials a call from Bristol to Edinburgh and speaks to the Lord Provost.
    - Prime Minister Harold Macmillan personally inspects and opens the United Kingdom's first ever motorway, the Preston Bypass, to traffic for the first time. The Bypass is now part of the M6 and M55 Motorways, and was significantly upgraded in the mid 1990s. 11 months later the M1, M45 and M10 Motorways open.
- December 9 – The right-wing John Birch Society is founded in the United States by Robert W. Welch, Jr., a retired candy manufacturer.
- December 14 – The *3rd Soviet Antarctic Expedition* becomes the first ever to reach the Southern Pole of Inaccessibility.

- December 15 – Arthur L. Schawlow and Charles H. Townes of Bell Laboratories publish a paper in *Physical Review Letters* setting out the principles of the optical laser.
- December 16 – A fire breaks out in the Vida Department Store in Bogotá, Colombia and kills 84 persons.
- December 18
  - The United States launches SCORE, the world's first communications satellite.
  - The Bell XV-3 Tiltrotor makes the first true mid-air transition from vertical helicopter-type flight to fully level fixed-wing flight.
- December 19 – A message from U.S. President Dwight D. Eisenhower is broadcast from the SCORE satellite.
- December 21 – General Charles de Gaulle is elected president of France with 78.5% of the votes.
- December 24 – 1958 BOAC Bristol Britannia crash: A BOAC Bristol Britannia (312 G-AOVD) crashes near Winkton, England during a test flight.
- December 25 – Tchaikovsky's ballet *The Nutcracker* (the George Balanchine version) is shown on prime-time television in color for the first time, as an episode of the CBS anthology series *Playhouse 90*.
- December 28 – In American football, the Baltimore Colts beat the New York Giants 23–17 to win the NFL Championship Game, the first to go into sudden death overtime and "The Greatest Game Ever Played".
- December 29 – Rebel troops under Che Guevara begin to invade Santa Clara, Cuba. Fulgencio Batista resigns two days later, on the night of the 31st.
- December 31 – Tallies reveal that, for the first time, the total of passengers carried by air this year exceeds the total carried by sea in transatlantic service.

Date unknown

- Nikita Khrushchev orders the Western allies to evacuate West Berlin within 6 months but backs down in the face of the Allies' unity.
- USA, USSR and Great Britain agree to stop testing atomic bombs for 3 years.
- During the International Geophysical Year, Earth's magnetosphere is discovered.
- The last legal female genital cutting occurs in the United States.
- Denatonium, the bitterest substance known, is discovered. It is used as an aversive agent in products such as bleach to reduce the risk of children drinking them.
- The Jim Henson Company is founded.
- Instant noodles go on sale for the first time.
- The Japanese 10 yen coin ceases having serrated edges after a 5-year period beginning in 1953. All 10 yen coins since have smooth edges.
- The British Rally Championship begins its first year.
- The University of New Orleans established
- Illinois observes the centennial of the Lincoln–Douglas debates.
- Sicilian writer Giuseppe Tomasi di Lampedusa's novel *Il Gattopardo* is published posthumously.
- Welsh cultural critic Raymond Williams publishes *Culture and Society*.
- Based on birth rates (per 1,000 population), the post-war baby boom ends in the United States as an 11-year decline in the birth rate begins (the longest on record in that country).
- The Professional Bowlers Tour is established at its headquarters in Seattle.

Births

January

Boris Tadić

Ellen DeGeneres

- January 1   Grandmaster Flash, African-American hip-hop/rap DJ
- January 2 – Vladimir Ovchinnikov, Russian pianist
- January 4
  - Matt Frewer, Canadian/American actor (*Max Headroom*)
  - James J. Greco, American businessman
  - Julian Sands, English actor
- January 9 – Mehmet Ali Ağca, Turkish militant, would-be assassin of Pope John Paul II

- January 11
    - Vicki Peterson, American rock musician (The Bangles)
    - Trevor Taylor, Jamaican-German singer and musician (Bad Boys Blue) (d. 2008)
- January 12 – Curt Fraser, American ice hockey coach
- January 13 – Ricardo Acuña, Chilean tennis player
- January 15 – Boris Tadić, Serbian president
- January 20
    - Lorenzo Lamas, American actor, martial artist and reality show participant
    - Masuo Amada, Japanese voice actor
- January 21 – Hussein Saeed Mohammed, Iraqi football player
- January 24 – Jools Holland, British musician
- January 26
    - Anita Baker, African-American soul and R&B singer
    - Ellen DeGeneres, American actress and comedian
- January 27 – Kadri Mälk, Estonian artist and jewelry designer
- January 29 – Stephen Lerner, American labor and community activist

February

Ice-T

Tim Kaine

- February 1 – Ryō Horikawa, Japanese voice actor
- February 4 – Tomasz Pacyński, Polish writer (d. 2005)
- February 8 – Sherri Martel, American professional wrestler (d. 2007)
- February 10 – Michael Weiss, jazz pianist and composer
- February 11
  - Michael Jackson, British broadcasting executive
  - Regina Maršíková, Czechoslovakian tennis player
- February 13 – Pernilla August, Swedish actress
- February 14
  - Grant Thomas, Australian rules footballer
  - Francisco Javier López Peña, Basque separatist
- February 16 – Ice-T, African-American rapper, songwriter, and actor
- February 19 – Steve Nieve, English musician
- February 20 – Jamal Hamdan, Lebanese actor and voice actor
- February 21
  - Jake Burns, Irish punk singer
  - Mary Chapin Carpenter, American singer
- February 25 – Kurt Rambis, American basketball player
- February 26
  - Susan Helms, American astronaut

- o Tim Kaine, American politician, U.S. Senator (D-Va.); 2016 Vice Presidential nominee under Hillary Clinton
- February 27 – Max Crivello, Italian artist
- February 28
  - o Natalya Estemirova, Russian activist (d. 2009)
  - o Phil Hayes, British voice actor

March

Miranda Richardson

Sharon Stone

Albert II, Prince of Monaco

Holly Hunter

Gary Oldman

- March 1 – Nik Kershaw, English singer
- March 3 – Miranda Richardson, English actress
- March 4 – Patricia Heaton, American actress
- March 5 – Andy Gibb, English-born singer (d. 1988)
- March 7
  - Rik Mayall, English comedian and actor (d. 2014)
  - Donna Murphy, American actress and singer
- March 8 – Gary Numan, British singer
- March 9
  - Linda Fiorentino, American actress
  - Mary Murphy, Dance choreographer
- March 10
  - Steve Howe, American baseball player (d. 2006)
  - Sharon Stone, American actress and producer
  - Hiroshi Yanaka, Japanese voice actor
- March 13 – Linda Robson, English actress

- March 14 – Albert II, Prince of Monaco
- March 15 – John Friedrich, American actor
- March 18
    - Kayo Hatta, American film director (d. 2005)
    - John Elefante, American singer and producer (*Kansas*)
- March 20 – Holly Hunter, American actress
- March 21 – Gary Oldman, English actor and filmmaker
- March 23 – Michael Sorich, American voice actor, actor, writer, director and voice director
- March 24 – Roland Koch, German politician
- March 25 – James McDaniel, American actor
- March 26 – Todd Joseph Miles Holden, American-born social scientist, author, basketball coach
- March 27 – Jessica Soho, Philippine television celebrity and reporter
- March 28
    - Bart Conner, American gymnast
    - Edesio Alejandro, Cuban music composer
    - Mr. Perfect, American professional wrestler (d. 2003)
- March 30 – Maurice LaMarche, Canadian voice actor
- March 31 – Dietmar Bartsch, German politician

April

Alec Baldwin

Andie MacDowell

Michelle Pfeiffer

- April 3 – Alec Baldwin, American actor and comedian
- April 4 – Cazuza, Brazilian poet, singer and composer (d. 1990)
- April 7 – Shinobu Adachi, Japanese voice actress
- April 10 – Yefim Bronfman, Russian-born pianist
- April 11
  - Hussniya Jabara, Israeli Arab politician
  - Luc Luycx, Belgian coin designer
- April 12 – Ginka Zagorcheva, Bulgarian athlete
- April 14
  - Peter Capaldi, Scottish actor
  - Junko Sakurada, Japanese actress and singer
- April 15
  - Keith Acton, Canadian ice hockey player and coach
  - Benjamin Zephaniah, British writer and musician

- April 21
  - Andie MacDowell, American actress
  - Yoshito Usui, Japanese manga artist (Crayon Shin-chan) (d. 2009)
- April 24 – Brian Paddick, British former deputy assistant commissioner and most senior openly gay police officer
- April 25
  - Fish, Scottish singer
  - Luis Guillermo Solís, President of Costa Rica
- April 26 – Ingolf Lück, German actor, comedian and television host
- April 28 – Hal Sutton, American golfer
- April 29
  - Michelle Pfeiffer, American actress
  - Eve Plumb, American actress

May

Annette Bening

- May 4 – Keith Haring, American artist (d. 1990)
- May 10 – Rick Santorum, former U.S. Senator
- May 11 – Christian Brando, American actor and eldest child of Marlon Brando (d. 2008)
- May 12
  - Dries van Noten, Belgian designer
  - Eric Singer, American rock drummer

- ○ Tony Oliver, American voice actor
- May 15 – Ron Simmons, American professional wrestler
- May 17 – Paul Whitehouse, Welsh actor, writer and comedian
- May 18 – Toyah Willcox, English actress & singer
- May 20 – Ron Reagan, political pundit and son of U.S. president Ronald Reagan
- May 21 – Tom Feeney, American Republican politician from the state of Florida
- May 23
  - ○ Mitch Albom, American author
  - ○ Drew Carey, American comedian and actor
  - ○ Lea DeLaria, American comedian and actress
- May 25
  - ○ Paul Weller, English singer-songwriter
  - ○ Carrie Newcomer, American singer-songwriter & musician
- May 26 – Margaret Colin, American actress
- May 26 – Moinul Ahsan Saber, Bangladeshi writer, editor.
- May 27
  - ○ Neil Finn, New Zealand singer and songwriter
  - ○ Linnea Quigley, American actress
- May 29
  - ○ Annette Bening, American actress
  - ○ Juliano Mer-Khamis, Israeli actor, director, filmmaker and political activist (d. 2011)
- May 30 – Marie Fredriksson, Swedish singer-songwriter

June

Prince

Bruce Campbell

- June 2 – Lex Luger, former American professional wrestler
- June 3 – Margot Käßmann, Lutheran theologian, German bishop
- June 4 – Gordon P. Robertson, American televangelist and son of Pat Robertson
- June 7 – Prince, African-American musician (d. 2016)
- June 8
  - Cyril O'Reilly, American actor
  - Keenen Ivory Wayans, African-American comedian, actor, and director
- June 12
  - Rebecca Holden, American actress, singer, and entertainer

- Meredith Brooks, American singer/songwriter and guitarist
- June 14
  - Masami Yoshida, Japanese athlete (d. 2000)
  - Eric Heiden, American speed skater
- June 15 – Wade Boggs, American baseball player
- June 17 – Jello Biafra, American punk musician and activist *(Dead Kennedys)*
- June 20
  - Chuck Wagner, American actor
  - Teiyū Ichiryūsai, Japanese voice actress
- June 22 – Bruce Campbell, American actor, producer, writer and director
- June 24 – John Tortorella, American ice hockey coach
- June 27 – Magnus Lindberg, Finnish composer
- June 28 – Félix Gray, French singer and songwriter
- June 29
  - Jeff Coopwood, American actor, broadcaster and singer
  - Rosa Mota, Portuguese long-distance runner
- June 30 – Esa-Pekka Salonen, Finnish conductor and composer

July

Kevin Bacon

Billy Mays

Kate Bush

Wong Kar-Wai

- July 2 – Thomas Bickerton, American Methodist bishop
- July 3 – Didier Mouron, Swiss artist
- July 5
  - Avigdor Lieberman, Israeli politician
  - Bill Watterson, American cartoonist (Calvin and Hobbes)
  - Kyoko Terase, Japanese voice actress
- July 6 – Jennifer Saunders, British comedian and actress
- July 7 – Michala Petri, Danish recorder player

- July 8
  - Kevin Bacon, American actor
  - Pauline Quirke, British actress
- July 15
  - Mac Thornberry, American politician
  - Austin Hayes, Irish footballer (d. 1986)
- July 16 – Michael Flatley, Irish-born dancer
- July 17 – Wong Kar-wai, Hong Kong second wave filmmaker
- July 19 – Azumah Nelson, Ghanaian boxer
- July 20 – Billy Mays, American infomercial salesperson (d. 2009)
- July 22 – Tatsunori Hara, Japanese professional-baseball coach and player
- July 27
  - Kimmo Hakola, Finnish composer
  - Margarethe Schreinemakers, German tlevision presenter
- July 28 – Terry Fox, Canadian athlete and cancer activist (d. 1981)
- July 30 – Kate Bush, English musician
- July 31 – Mark Cuban, American entrepreneur and basketball team owner

August

Madonna

Angela Bassett

Belinda Carlisle

Steve Guttenberg

Tim Burton

Michael Jackson

- August 1 – Adrian Dunbar, Irish actor and director
- August 2 – Shō Hayami, Japanese voice actor and singer
- August 7
  - Bruce Dickinson, English musician (Iron Maiden)
  - Russell Baze, Canadian/American champion jockey
- August 10
  - Don Swayze, American actor
  - Rami Hamdallah, Palestine politician
- August 15
  - Victor Shenderovich, Russian writer
  - Chiharu Suzuka, Japanese voice actress
- August 16
  - Madonna, American-born singer, songwriter, and actress
  - Angela Bassett, African-American actress
- August 17 – Belinda Carlisle, American singer
- August 19 – Anthony Muñoz, American football player
- August 20 – Nicholas Bell, English actor based in Australia
- August 22 – Colm Feore, American-born actor
- August 24 – Steve Guttenberg, American actor
- August 25 – Tim Burton, American film director
  - Christian LeBlanc, American actor
- August 27 – Normand Brathwaite, African-Canadian comedian and television and radio host
- August 29 – Michael Jackson, African-American singer, songwriter and dancer (d. 2009)

September

Jeff Foxworthy

Stevie Vallance

Kevin Sorbo

- September 6
  - Jeff Foxworthy, American comedian, actor, author
  - Sione Vailahi, Tongan professional wrestler ("The Barbarian")

- September 8
  - Mitsuru Miyamoto, Japanese voice actor
  - Reiko Terashima, Japanese manga artist and illustrator
  - Stevie Vallance, Canadian actress, voice actress, stage performer, singer, casting director and voice director
- September 9 – Colin Murdock, Canadian voice actor
- September 10
  - Chris Columbus (filmmaker), American film director/writer/producer
  - Siobhan Fahey, Irish singer (Bananarama, Shakespears Sister)
- September 11 – Julia Nickson-Soul, Singapore actress
- September 13 – Paweł Przytocki, Polish conductor
- September 14
  - Michael Bollner, German actor
  - Jeff Crowe, New Zealand cricketer
- September 15 – Anne Davies, British television presenter and newsreader
- September 16
  - Orel Hershiser, American baseball player
  - Jennifer Tilly, Canadian/American actress
- September 19 – Lita Ford, British musician
- September 21 – Bruno Fitoussi, French poker player
- September 22
  - Andrea Bocelli, Italian tenor
  - Joan Jett, American rock musician
- September 23 – Marvin Lewis, American football coach
- September 24 – Kevin Sorbo, American actor
- September 25
  - Michael Madsen, American actor
  - Eamonn Healy, Irish chemist
- September 26 – Darby Crash, American rock songwriter, singer (Germs) (d. 1980)

- September 27 – Irvine Welsh, Scottish writer
- September 29 – Tom Buhrow, German journalist and intendant of the WDR
- September 30 – Marty Stuart, American singer

October

Tim Robbins

Viggo Mortensen

- October 3 – Chen Yanyin, Chinese sculptor
- October 4 – Ned Luke, American actor
- October 5 – Neil deGrasse Tyson, American astrophysicist and science communicator (Also host of many episodes of NOVA)
- October 8 – Ursula von der Leyen, German politician who has been the Minister of Defence
- October 14
  - Thomas Dolby, English rock musician
  - Peter Kloeppel, German television journalist
- October 15 – Masako Katsuki, Japanese voice actress

- October 16 – Tim Robbins, American actor
- October 17 – Alan Jackson, American country singer and songwriter
- October 20
  - Mark King, English singer and musician (Level 42)
  - Viggo Mortensen, American actor
  - Scott Hall, American professional wrestler
- October 23 – Hiroyuki Kinoshita, Japanese actor and voice actor
- October 25
  - Phil Daniels, English actor
  - Kornelia Ender, German swimmer
- October 27 – Simon Le Bon, English rock singer
- October 29 – Blažej Baláž, Slovak painter

November

Jamie Lee Curtis

- November 2 – Willie McGee, African-American baseball player
- November 8 – Jeff Speakman, American actor and martial artist
- November 10 – Vicky Rosti, Finnish singer, former Eurovision contestant

- November 12
  - Megan Mullally, American actress, singer and media personality
  - Hiromi Iwasaki, Japanese singer
- November 16
  - Marg Helgenberger, American actress
  - Boris Krivokapić, Serbian academic
- November 17 – Mary Elizabeth Mastrantonio, American actress and singer
- November 18 – Laura Miller, Mayor of Dallas, Texas
- November 19 – Michael Wilbon, American sportswriter
- November 21 – David Reivers, Jamaican actor
- November 22
  - Jamie Lee Curtis, American actress
  - Bruce Payne, English actor and producer
- November 25 – Darlanne Fluegel, American actress
- November 27 – Tetsuya Komuro, Japanese music producer and songwriter
- November 28 – Dave Righetti, American baseball player
- November 30 – Juliette Bergmann, Dutch bodybuilder

December

- December 1
  - Charlene Tilton, American actress
  - Javier Aguirre, Mexican football player and manager
- December 2 – Mina Asami, Japanese actress
- December 5 – Dynamite Kid, English professional wrestler
- December 6
  - Nick Park, English filmmaker and animator
  - Debbie Rowe, American ex-wife of pop star Michael Jackson, and mother of two of his children
- December 10 – Cornelia Funke, German author

- December 11 – Nikki Sixx, American rock musician
- December 12
  - Monica Attard, Australian journalist
  - Lucie Guay, Canadian canoer
  - Dag Ingebrigtsen, Norwegian musician
  - Sheree J. Wilson, American actress
- December 13 – Lynn-Holly Johnson, American ice skater and actress
- December 14
  - Mike Scott, Scottish singer-songwriter (The Waterboys)
  - Spider Stacy, English musician (The Pogues)
  - François Zocchetto, French politician
- December 18 – Julia Wolfe, American composer
- December 19 – Limahl, English singer
- December 21 – Kevin Blackwell, English football manager
- December 25
  - Dimi Mint Abba, Mauritanian musician and singer (d. 2011)
  - Hanford Dixon, American football player
  - Rickey Henderson, African-American baseball player
  - Alannah Myles, Canadian singer-songwriter
- December 26 – Mieko Harada, Japanese actress
- December 28 – Twila Paris, American Christian musician
- December 29 – Lakhdar Belloumi, Algerian football player
- December 31 – Bebe Neuwirth, American actress

Date unknown

- Helena Klakocar, Dutch cartoonist
- Yoshiteru Otani, Japanese cartoonist

Deaths

January

- January 1 – Edward Weston, American photographer (b. 1886)
- January 4 – Archie Alexander, American designer/governor (b. 1888)
- January 7 – Margaret Anglin, stage actress (b. 1876)
- January 8 – Paul Pilgrim, American athlete (b. 1883)
- January 9 – Karl Reinhardt, German philologist. (b. 1886)
- January 11 – Edna Purviance, American actress (b. 1895)
- January 13 – Jesse L. Lasky, American film producer (b. 1880)
- January 16 – Aubrey Mather, English actor (b. 1885)
- January 19 – Cândido Rondon, Brazilian military officer (b. 1865)
- January 20 – Ataúlfo Argenta, Spanish conductor and pianist (b. 1913)
- January 30
  - Jean Crotti, Swiss artist (b. 1878)
  - Ernst Heinkel, German aircraft designer and manufacturer (b. 1888)

February

- February 1 – Clinton Davisson, American physicist, Nobel Prize laureate (b. 1888)
- February 2 – Walter Kingsford, English actor (b. 1881)
- February 4
  - Monta Bell, American actor (b. 1891)
  - Henry Kuttner, American author (b. 1915)

- February 6
  - Geoff Bent (b. 1932)
  - Roger Byrne (b. 1929)
  - Eddie Colman (b. 1936)
  - Mark Jones (b. 1933)
  - David Pegg (b. 1935)
  - Tommy Taylor (b. 1932)
  - Liam "Billy" Whelan (b. 1935), all footballers that perished in the Munich air disaster
- February 10 – Aleksander Klumberg, Estonian decathlete (b. 1899)
- February 13
  - Christabel Pankhurst, English suffragette (b. 1880)
  - Georges Rouault, French painter (b. 1871)
  - Helen Twelvetrees, American actress (b. 1908)
- February 16 – Situ Qiao, Chinese painter (b. 1902)
- February 17 – Marguerite Snow, American actress (b. 1889)
- February 20 – Thurston Hall, American actor (b. 1882)
- February 21 – Duncan Edwards English footballer (b. 1936), injury in the Munich air disaster
- February 27 – Harry Cohn, American film producer (b. 1891)

March

- March 11 – Princess Ingeborg of Denmark (b. 1878)
- March 20 – Adegoke Adelabu, Nigerian politician (b. 1915) (car crash)
- March 21 – Cyril M. Kornbluth, American writer (b. 1923)
- March 22 (in plane crash)
  - Mike Todd, American film producer (b. 1909)
  - Art Cohn, American screenwriter (b. 1909)

- March 23 – Charlotte Walker, American actress (b. 1876)
- March 24 – Herbert Fields, American librettist and screenwriter (b. 1897)
- March 25 – Tom Brown, American musician (b. 1888)
- March 26 – Phil Mead, English cricketer (b. 1887)
- March 28
  - W. C. Handy, African-American blues composer (b. 1873)
  - Chuck Klein, American baseball player (Philadelphia Phillies) and a member of the MLB Hall of Fame (b. 1904)

April

- April 2
  - Willie Maley, Scottish football player and manager (b. 1868)
  - Jōsei Toda, Japanese educator and activist (b. 1900)
- April 8
  - George Jean Nathan, American drama critic (b. 1882)
  - Frank Eaton, American U.S. Deputy Marshal (b. 1860)
- April 15 – Estelle Taylor, American actress (b. 1894)
- April 16 – Rosalind Franklin, British crystallographer (b. 1920)
- April 18 – Maurice Gamelin, French general (b. 1872)
- April 19 – Billy Meredith, Welsh footballer (b. 1874)

May

- May 2 – Henry Cornelius, South African-born director (b. 1913)
- May 3 – Frank Foster, English cricketer (b. 1889)
- May 5 – James Branch Cabell, American writer (b. 1879)

- May 7 – Mihkel Lüdig, Estonian composer, organist and choir conductor (b. 1880)
- May 18 – Jacob Fichman, Israeli poet and essayist (b. 1881)
- May 19 – Ronald Colman, English actor (b. 1891)
- May 26 – Constantin Cantacuzino, Romanian aviator (b. 1905)
- May 29 – Juan Ramón Jiménez, Spanish writer, Nobel Prize laureate (b. 1881)

June

Imre Nagy

Kurt Alder

- June 2 – Townsend Cromwell, American oceanographer (plane crash) (b. 1922)
- June 6
  - Lloyd Hughes, American actor (b. 1897)
  - Virginia Pearson, American actress (b. 1886)
- June 9 – Robert Donat, English actor (b. 1905)
- June 13 – Edwin Keppel Bennett, British writer (b. 1887)

- June 16
  - Alexander Chervyakov, Prime Minister of the Byelorussian SSR (suicide) (b. 1892)
  - Imre Nagy, former Prime Minister of Hungary (executed) (b. 1896)
  - Nereu Ramos, 20th President of Brazil (b. 1888)
- June 20 – Kurt Alder, German chemist, Nobel Prize laureate (b. 1902)
- June 21
  - Herbert Brenon, American film director (b. 1880)
  - Robert L. Ghormley, American admiral (b. 1883)
- June 26 – George Orton, Canadian athlete (b. 1876)
- June 28 – Alfred Noyes, English poet (b. 1880)

July

- July 2 – Martha Boswell, American singer (b. 1905)
- July 3 – Charles Bathurst, 1st Viscount Bledisloe, English politician, 4th Governor-General of New Zealand (b. 1867)
- July 9 – James H. Flatley, American naval aviator and admiral (b. 1906)
- July 14 (killed during *coup d'état*):
  - King Faisal II of Iraq (b. 1935)
  - 'Abd al-Ilah, former regent of Iraq (b. 1913)
- July 15 – Julia Lennon, English mother of John Lennon (b. 1914)
- July 18 – Henri Farman, pioneer French aviator and aircraft company founder (b. 1874)
- July 20 – Franklin Pangborn, American actor (b. 1889)
- July 24 – Mabel Ballin, American actress (b. 1887)
- July 25 – Harry Warner, American studio executive (b. 1881)

- July 26 – Iven Carl Kincheloe, Jr., American Korean War fighter ace and test pilot (b. 1928)
- July 27 – Claire Lee Chennault, American aviator and general, leader of the Flying Tigers (b. 1893)
- July 30 – William A. Glassford, American admiral (b. 1886)

August

Ernest Lawrence

- August 3 – Peter Collins, Formula 1 driver (b. 1931)
- August 8 – Barbara Bennett, American actress (b. 1906)
- August 14
  - Frédéric Joliot-Curie, French physicist, recipient of the Nobel Prize in Chemistry (b. 1900)
  - Gladys Presley, American, mother of Elvis Presley (b. 1912)
- August 16 – Paul Panzer, German actor (b. 1872)
- August 18 – Bonar Colleano, American actor (b. 1924)
- August 22 – Roger Martin du Gard, French writer, Nobel Prize laureate (b. 1881)
- August 24 – Paul Henry, Northern Irish artist (b. 1876)
- August 26 – Ralph Vaughan Williams, English composer (b. 1872)
- August 27 – Ernest Lawrence, American physicist, Nobel Prize laureate (b. 1901)

- August 29 – Marjorie Flack, American artist, illustrator and writer (b. 1897)

September

- September 11
  - Hans Grundig, German artist (b. 1901)
  - Robert W. Service, Scottish-born Canadian poet (b. 1874)
- September 16 – Alma Bennett, American actress (b. 1904)
- September 23
  - Alfred Piccaver, British-American operatic tenor (b. 1884)
  - Walter Friedrich Otto, German classical philologist (b. 1874)
- September 25 – John B. Watson, American psychologist (b. 1878)

October

Pope Pius XII

- October 9 – Pope Pius XII (b. 1876)
- October 11 – Maurice de Vlaminck, French painter (b. 1876)
- October 17
  - Charlie Townsend, English cricketer (b. 1876)
  - Paul Outerbridge American photographer (b. 1896)

- October 14 – Douglas Mawson, Australian geologist and polar explorer (b. 1882)
- October 15 – Jack Norton, American actor (b. 1882)
- October 16 – Michalis Souyioul, Greek composer (b. 1906)
- October 24 – G. E. Moore, British philosopher of (*Principia Ethica*) (b. 1873)
- October 27 – Marshall Neilan, American actor and director (b. 1891)
- October 29 – Zoë Akins, American playwright, poet and author (b. 1886)

November

Tyrone Power

- November 15
  - Samuel Hopkins Adams, American writer (b. 1871)
  - Tyrone Power, American actor (b. 1914)
- November 19 – Vittorio Ambrosio, Italian general (b. 1879)
- November 21 – Mel Ott, American baseball player (New York Giants) and a member of the MLB Hall of Fame (b. 1909)
- November 24
  - Robert Cecil, 1st Viscount Cecil of Chelwood, English politician and diplomat, recipient of the Nobel Peace Prize (b. 1864)
  - Harry Parke, American comedian (b. 1904)

- November 27 – Artur Rodziński, Polish conductor (b. 1892)
- November 30 – Oscar C. Badger II, American admiral (b. 1890)

December

Wolfgang Pauli

- December 1 – Boots Mallory, American actress (b. 1913)
- December 8 – Tris Speaker, American baseball player (Cleveland Indians) and a member of the MLB Hall of Fame (b. 1888)
- December 12
    - Albert Walsh, Lieutenant Governor of Newfoundland (b. 1900)
    - Milutin Milanković, Serbian mathematician, astronomer, climatologist and geophysicist, (b. 1879)
- December 13 – Tim Moore, American comedian (b. 1887)
- December 15 – Wolfgang Pauli, Austrian-born physicist, Nobel Prize laureate (b. 1900)
- December 21
    - H. B. Warner, English actor (b. 1875)
    - Lion Feuchtwanger, German novelist and playwright (b. 1884)
- December 27 – Mustafa Merlika-Kruja, 13rd Prime Minister of Albania (b. 1887)

- December 29 – Doris Humphrey, American dancer and choreographer (b. 1895)

Date unknown

- Stylianos Lykoudis, Greek admiral (b. 1878)
- Thomas Chrostwaite, American educator (b. 1873)

Nobel Prizes

- Physics – Pavel Alekseyevich Cherenkov, Ilya Mikhailovich Frank, and Igor Yevgenyevich Tamm
- Chemistry – Frederick Sanger
- Physiology or Medicine – George Wells Beadle, Edward Lawrie Tatum, and Joshua Lederberg
- Literature – Boris Leonidovich Pasternak
- Peace – Georges Pire

Media

- In Stephen King's novel *11/22/63*, the time bubble in Al's Diner sends the protagonist Jake Epping to 11:58 AM on the morning of September 9, 1958.

In the News

NASA National Aeronautics and Space Administration is formed.

The U.S. launches the Explorer 1 satellite.

14 year old Bobby Fischer wins the United States Chess Championship.

The Munich Air Disaster occurs after a plane crashes carrying the Manchester United team.

Sir Edmund Hillary reaches the South Pole.

Elvis Presley is inducted into the Army.

Brazil wins the **1958** World Cup in Sweden.

US Nuclear Submarine " Nautilus " passes under Ice Cap at North Pole.

Popular Films - The Bridge on the River Kwai, South Pacific, Gigi, King Creole, Vertigo.

Popular TV Programmes - Candid Camera, The Ed Sullivan Show, Come Dancing, The Jack Benny Show, Panorama, Alfred Hitchcock Presents.

General Charles de Gaulle becomes Prime Minister of France.

Nikita Khrushchev becomes Premier of the Soviet Union.

Nelson Rockefeller Elected Governor of New York.